# Dawn; I'm The Villain In This One

By: Antwoun Stevens

# Contents

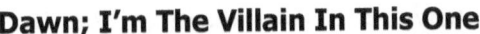

**Dedicated to Immanuel Cordell Stevens
I Love You Son**

# Prologue

"Dawn"

Somewhere between midnight and death he lays in a pile of his own vomit. Face planted and barely breathing, he is way too drunk to move yet, this is the quietest his mind has been since he could remember.

If Jack Daniels and depression has taught me anything it is this; there are two things that are definite in this world. The first, being that we all will fall in love. Let it be a person, place, or thing. It is an overwhelming experience that consumes your entire being; a feeling of something "belonging" to you. The second is that we all will die. In that moment on my bathroom floor I was came to the realization of both. I laid there in my own vomit romanticizing the idea of death, while reminiscing over the feeling of butterflies flying in the pits of my stomach. Neither concept was new to me. Being a knight in shining armor has always been a dream of mine. I've always wanted to sweep a woman off her feet and make her feel something that only movies are made of. And when it comes to death, the Grim Reaper and I have been acquainted since as long as I can remember. The first time I met him I believed in his offer and thought that he had my best interest at heart. When I was in the third grade I told my teacher, I wanted to kill myself. That was the first time that I understood the power of words. Since then the Grim Reaper and I have been playing tug-a-war with the idea of existing and the loudness of silence. You were the only thing to ever make sense. The only thing that helped me believe in anything. You were Home.

# Dear Dark Skinned Women

I like all women
I mean tall women
Short women
Thick women
Round women
Middle Eastern women
Hispanic women
Asian women
And of course – of course you

**Dear Dark Skinned women**
You got that I know I got it attitude
That boy you want it you better need it attitude
That Ethiopian queen attitude
Plain and simple baby girl - you got an attitude
But whenever you smile pieces of my soul get caught in the
corners of your grin

**Dear Dark Skinned Women**
Whenever you laugh my heart melts into a lake of forbidden
tears

**Dear Dark Skinned Women**
Your footsteps sound like trumpets playing whenever the walls
of Jericho fell when you tip toe across my bedroom

**Dear Dark Skinned Women**
I apologize for societies ignorance
But you must understand
Intimidation causes imitation that's why so many people want
to be like you

**Dear Dark Skinned Women**
I apologize on the behalf of me and my ignorant brothers
That make you fill up with that Malcom X anger before he went
to mecca

And when you see me you ask me to leave with those Marcus Garvey eyes

**Dear Dark Skinned Women**
You have the strength of slaves in your heels
Bessie Coleman in your thighs
You're so strong you can stand your ground while sitting you got Rosa Parks in your spine
Etta James in your voice
Coretta Scott King in your smile
Sojourner Truth in your eyes
And Madam CJ Walkers' hot comb that got that hair slick down to the side

**Dear Dark Skinned women**
Most men will tell you that they want to be your knight in shining armor
But me
I want to be your hype man on your lowest days
I want to help the cheek bones in your face express your smile
Most men will tell you that they want to make love to you
But me
I want to make your eyes roll down your spine and make you see why I fell in love with you in the first place

**Dear Dark Skinned Women**
Most men will tell you that you give them butterflies
But me
You create fire breathing dragons in the pits of my stomach

**Dear Dark Skinned Women**
Most men will tell you that they cherish you
But me
I pray that one day I will be able to give birth nations that will create monuments in your name
Just -
To remember you

**Dear Dark Skinned Women**
The Mona Lisa couldn't even compare to your shadow
You were sculpted out with hands of passion
No matter what anybody has ever said about you

**Dear Dark Skinned Women**
You are beautiful

## Dear Immanuel, 17SEP18

We went to the doctors' office today
You had to get a couple of shots
You stripped down to nothing but your diaper
And you insisted on wearing my hat
You cried like a baby
But after a couple of crackers you sucked it up
And ate through the pain
What a soldier of a boy

## Handyman

I am bad at a lot of things
Take cooking for an example
I burn toast
No, not the scrap it off burnt toast
I'm talking about fire alarm damn what were you doing burnt
toast
I'm bad at math. Like I'm not good in Algebra, Calculus,
Trigonometry, Addition, Multiplication, Division, and
occasionally Subtraction.
BUT
You know what I'm really good at?
I'm really good at being a Handyman
Because I have a habit of mending shattered hearts without
wearing gloves
Cutting open wounds of my own leaving them to become
infected
My heart becomes WD-40 to rusty bolts called love until I'm
down to the last drop
I have a tendency of getting ripped off by the demons she
calls the "The Truth" until my pockets are empty
I have a confession
I foolishly love blind

## Sweet/Sexy/Savage - Reasons Why I Love Kehlani

I

As the president of Kehlani's fan club I would like to introduce to you all this
An ode to our queen
Whose favorite color is blue
Who loves to eat Italian food
And whose skin is as strong as a diamond and heart as soft as jellyfish
I - Antwoun Stevens have vowed to protect her
You see she is fearless
Equipped with a voice that literally shakes stadiums
People come and sing her name in unison
You can correlate her energy to that of supernovas
She is Aset, Isis, and Mary all in one
Everything that you could ask the creator for in a woman

II

She warned us all on "Do You Dirty"
Told me not to fall in love but of course thou shall not listen
I am a Viking determined to be one even with the fiercest dragons
She is my night fury

III

That Bay Area swagger ya dig
The way her style screams her name
Showing those ravishing curves and legs that could uproot a nation to defend them
She treats every room she walks in as if she is moon walking across the Golden Gate bridge
She is full of might

IV

Her confidence is enticing
Every picture she posts on social media she is serving us fierce

Demonstrating that no matter what life throws at us we are still giants amongst it
That depression will never get the best of us
All we have to do is swing one more time
Before the knock out

## V
Those Tattoos
Marked with the inks of the goddess
She is a mural of black girl magic
Showing the world that art comes in all shades
And that even her glance could over power that of a Da Vinci painting

## VI
That attitude
She is a bag of sass ready to be unleashed on any mere mortal who dares to challenge her existence
She shows us that femininity is a necessity in balancing masculinity
She is the Luna to my Sol
There would be no purpose in me shinning without her

## VII
Ok so I have a confession
I am not the president of Kehlani's fan club
I am not sure if her favorite color is blue, but I know that yours is
I don't know if she loves eating Italian food, but I know that you do
That your skin is as hard as a diamond and your heart is as soft as a jellyfish
That you are Aset, Isis, and Mary all in one
That you are the Luna to my Sol
That there is no purpose in me shining without you
You see the real reason why I love Kehlani
Is because since you left
Listening to her music helps me feel
As if I'm still next to you

## Listening

I stared into the night sky and listened to the darkness.
He spoke to me of many things.
I told him that I missed your glow
And in return he brightens the moon and it reminded me of
your skin
I told him that I missed your smile
And in that moment a shooting star carried it across the
skyline
I told him that I missed your laughter
And the ocean overheard our conversation and brought it to
me on a wave
And then the wind brought me the comfort of your lips
And the earth herself sang like rhythm and blues
And I waltz with the loneliness that once filled my heart
And I dropped to my knees
And I prayed
I prayed that reincarnation is real
Just in case I die before you do
So that I can be born again as one of your heartbeats
Because I would sacrifice a lifespan so brief
Just so that I can experience what it's like to really
Be
Inside of you

## She's not you

I tried to fuck the memory of you out of my mind
But her moans didn't sound like yours
And her back just wouldn't arch like yours does
And my hands couldn't find home wrapped around her hair
like they do in yours
I guess that's why I thought about you after

## Dear Immanuel, 8APR18

Today I made it to New York
You were with your mother for the weekend
Your Aunt, you, and I all went down to the World Trade Center memorial
To think how they honored the chaos that once was
People were smiling everywhere
Remembering the love that once existed
And we were no different

## Stupid

I don't know what's scarier
The fact that you may not know how much I truly care about you
Or that you do and that's why you haven't acknowledged it

## Reality

A Promise is a comfort to a fool

## Why Now?

Why are you trying to love me now?
Why do u give a fuck about me now?
You haven't given a fuck about me in a long time.
Did u ever really care about me?
Or is it the fact that I was somebody to put your problems off
on
To blame me for everything wrong in your life
Why are you trying to be sweet and kind now?
Where was all of this when we were together?
Why did it take me to leave for you to acknowledge the
importance of my fucking existence in the first place?
Do u even mean anything you are doing?
Is hurting me all just a big game to you?
Quit emailing me about how you are praying for me and ready
to co-parent.
You barely even believe in god
You manipulate me
You lie to me
You have to still lying to me
Right?
Is it all of my fault?
Do I deserve this because of past choices I've made?
Is this karma?
Is this what it feels likes to feel toyed with?
I tried to love you
I gave you my all
It wasn't enough
Why is my love never enough?

## Dear Immanuel 20AUG19

Your mother FaceTimed me today and I got to see you play
on the playground for the first time
You don't let challenges stop you
Nothing hinders you form being great
You were filled with so much joy
So much happiness
And for the first time today
I laughed
And meant it

## Thoughts

I died for you every day since I could remember
Every morning I would put to rest a me that the world needs
not
And I would bury it deep beneath my eyelids
That's why I stare whenever I look at you
Because if I blink
For even a second the nightmares will come
And you would only be a dream
You were only a dream
I rested my thoughts on the pelvis of your mind
I fiddled with your heart afraid that I would break it
And I did
I always do
My pride usually bulldozes anything good that gives birth in
my path
You were no exception
I stare at my phone contemplating rather to contact you or let
you be
I always conclude to let you be
Because deep down I know
You'll be best without me
Some of us are meant to build castles but not really live in
them
So, I will watch from afar
As you become happy
Again

# I AM

I
I am an eight note on an intangible measure called life
A song with a none existent rest and a B flat melody
My words are dream catchers and follow my shadows in the
REM of sleep
My soul is a half note because the other half is missing
My heart pumps whole notes to make for the lack there of
I am still my favorite song

## Dear Immanuel, 28DEC17

Today I made it home to you from deployment
I held you for the first time
I was smiling from ear to ear
I was happy to just be
With you

## 10 Reasons Why You Should Never Love Me (*Circa 2011*)

1. Because your voice sounds like dragon flies fluttering the shallow canals of my closed earlobes
2. I'm overwhelmed by my dangerous feelings
I'm incapable of talking about my emotions
I become mime filed with the inability to speak
Because I don't like how it feels to be vulnerable
3. My heart is shattered on a marble floor of broken dreams where ghosts of relationships past are practicing their pirouettes before their next victim.
4. I don't think I can fall in love again.
5. Because I grabbed cupid by his throat and shoved down every arrow he's ever shot at me
And told him
"If he ever did it again I was going to call God and file a complaint for dangerous use of a deadly weapon"
6. Have you ever watched the sunset?
The way sunlight lowers its head to darkness
I still wonder if it inhabits her smile
7. I like to think that it still does.
8. You can still produce butterflies
9. My stomach is filled with pesticides making them die before they get their wings
10. Because I can't love you like you deserve.
11. Because your arms are stretched out like willow branches on an autumn eve night
But me I'm unable to reach.
Unable to Speak
Unable to even count for that matter
1. Because your voice sounds like dragon flies fluttering the shallow canals of my closed earlobe
And I -
And I am not ready to listen

## Small Regrets

I wish I never wished I never
Then maybe regrets wouldn't fill my insides like dead
caterpillars who never got to see their full potential
Leaving the soul with a feeling of collapsing emptiness
I wish I never wished I never
Then the sunrise could just be the sunrise
The sunset could just be the sunset
Moonlight could just shine and be moonlight
I wish I never wished I never
Then maybe time wouldn't chase me down dark alley ways
and beat me senseless
Turning my sweet dreams into bitter nightmares
Making me resent the sound of humming birds for what it
resembles to me
I wish I never wished I never
Then words like "Regret" wouldn't taste like dead meat on the
tip of my tongue
I wish that I didn't wish at all
Only to have experienced
And to have lived

## Love

Love isn't just a four-letter word that sounds good to say
Love is the pursuit of happiness
Resulting in life changing moments with the most fruitful of
outcomes
Love glides on the taste buds of such fragile creatures
Love is for the eyes to hear
And the ears to see
Love is for the hands to beat
And the heart to feel
Love is for the feet to evaporate
And the soul to walk
Love is a four-letter word
A foreword letter to you; Is love

# If God Gave Second Chances (*Circa 2013*)

Your Skin felt like vines wrapped around this abandoned
house because no heart is present in a broken home
I thought you were a gardener
Ripping out the weeds in the cracks of "I told you so's and
What If's"
You had a green thumb
You planted these seeds inside of me
And gave creation to roses
But somehow you forgot to clip the thrones
And whenever I inhale the pollen burns my throat
Lately it has been impossible for me to blossom
You promised me that your feeling were permanent
Rooted into the soil of your soul
But instead they were like daises
Breath taking at first but no matter how much I seemed to
water them
They always seem to die
I told myself that if I closed my eyes everything would be ok
But when I awoke I found myself a victim of infidelity
I thought you were done sleeping with your insecurities
Some days I still play back our first kiss
You stood at 5 feet
Long hair resting on the sides of your cheeks
Your eyes were the same color as your thumbs
And they always changed color
Like the leaves when the seasons breezed through our
hometown
I was only 6'2
It should have taken Albert Einstein himself to come up with a
formula for our lips to lock
But God was out Scientist
He put an arch in my back and wings underneath your feet
And for the first time in my life
I could have sworn that I understood Algebra
I was at peace
I had found pure happiness

We got to fully experience each other
And some days I sit and think about you
And I wonder
If God gives second chances

## Dear Immanuel 3JUN17

Your mother sent me pictures of your sonogram this today
Your head is enormous
Just like your fathers
I know at this point that she is going to have a long day when
you come

## The Flamingo (*Circa 2011*)

She is as elegant as a flamingo
As she stands on the tip of her toes weightless on the ballroom floor
As if she was standing in a pond of fear
She twirls
As if every footing was life or death
Success or failure
As she thinks of nothing but her dreams of dancing in front of an audience
She jumps
And the glare from the sun shinning through the window shows pure determination in her luscious mirrors that us humans call eyes
Then she lands
Perfectly
Then I approach her as if I was a planet and she was the sun
Her gravitational pull of serenity
I put my hand out in hopes that she would do the same
Creating a connection of vibrations as African drums and chants echo from the background as our ancestors rejoice in unison
I take the lead
As we move step by step
Foot by foot
Mind by Body
Soul by Soul
The sound of her laughter unleashes my form of her heaven from her throat
I smile
Showing her assurance as we dance
Without any music
However, it was still as smooth and crisp as her idols
I tell her to close her eyes and imagine
She's now in an extravagant dress and I'm in an old school zoot suit
We move to the sound of jazz playing in a New Orleans night club

I tell her to close her eyes and imagine
The sound of hip hop playing as we dance effortlessly in an
Atlanta prom dance
I tell her to close her eyes and imagine
The sound of lions as the sunsets
And we move hand and hand in her pond of fear
The elegance of a dancer who is as balanced as a flamingo
And an eagle with a dream of flight
And the heart
The heart of a man

## A Dreamers Eulogy

When we die
The quantity of people who loved us will be an after thought
Only the quality will remain
Our souls will never remember the people who liked our
pictures
However
They will always be tied to those whose eyes still hold a
picture of our souls
Those are the people worth living for

## We are Whole

I hear heart beats
Each pound against chest reminds the body that you are still
alive
It encourages the lungs to take another breathe
Forcing the brain to operate
And to tell the legs to "Just keep moving"
I feel the wind skim across my skin
Its not from the shoreline but from the current produced by
lover's eyes
I see you
For everything that is beautiful in this world
I taste happiness
It crawls into my mouth every time I say that I love you
And it keeps reminding me
That we are whole

## Dear Immanuel 13AUG19

Today we talked on the phone for 30 mins
I watched you color your homework
In your own little way, you were like Picasso
You fell and started crying out for daddy
But you weren't calling out for me
You were calling out to him
And then you picked up the phone and asked who I was
As if I wouldn't die for you

# In The Morning (*Circa 2014*)

Bodies Crashing like Waves on shorelines
Every stroke like a renaissance painting
Back and forth back and forth
Sighs of relief
Nails into back
As if trying to claw away at the pain of the week
Sweat dripping
Legs shaking
Back aching
Sweat dripping
Legs shaking
Back aching
Sweat dripping
Legs shaking
Back aching
And then - we collapse
Souls lost in each other for the moment
Locking eyes but not saying a single word
Yet knowing everything that needs to be heard
Thighs beaten into the mattress to make sure that you
remember me
As being more than just a man
But the idea that brought you a couple hours of pleasure
And peace

## Rose

How do you measure out sorrow?
How do you feel pure agony for something you loved so
deeply but never got to experience?
To speak to
To Hold
After the second miscarriage of my life
I did not cry
I did not feel anger
Wasn't consumed by sadness
I felt numb
Not really knowing what but knowing that something
unexplainable was felt
I couldn't put that feeling into words
I thought that my silence was loud enough for you to
understand
That you heard the bombs dropping too
You cried tears that I never got to wipe away
And instead of me crying with you I decided to be your rock
To be the boulder for you to lean on
The foundation in which I thought you would find your peace
But it only helped in creating your solitude
Meanwhile I buried my pain deep inside of me
You asked me about it, but I never spoke on it
How could I?
How dare I have the audacity to heal?
We created life together
But when it died I wasn't there
I was hundreds of miles away
The weight of no longer carrying weight you had to hold
Alone
Who was I to be sad?
But -
But you needed that from me
Needed to see that I was hurting too
But all I knew was that you needed me
But you needed to see that I needed you too
And since that day we only know how to speak in fire

Our conversations were once like a cathedral
We found home in on our darkest days
Now everything is in enflamed all around us
Some days I still picture our daughter running to me
screaming "Daddy"
And every time I do she has your eyes
Your smile
Your sass
Most days I wake up and ask my self
"How do you go from thinking you were going to spend the
rest of your life with someone"
To knowing
That you will never get to hold them again

# Dear Immanuel 3FEB18

There was a photoshoot that took place for you
In the photo I smiled from ear to ear
I held you and you looked like you were confused
As if you felt my own inner conflict
Do I suffer my happiness for you?
Or will my search for happiness cause you to suffer?
Am I doing the right thing?

## Lovehall Session (The First time)

She arrived
In wedges
My arch nemesis
Rage filled my mind
But I forgave the hate crime against style and she walked in
And my god was she beautiful
A beautiful dress that drove against her curves
Legs oozing of Aphrodite
And a grin big enough to build a life upon
I was prepared for a romantic evening
Fine cuisine that I tried to get her to believe that I cooked
myself
But after one bite she knew it was ordered in
We laughed
Music echoing from the speaker
We danced
Cheesy, I know but we both find something worth feeling in
that moment
We headed to the bedroom were rose petals awaited
She undressed
Showing her bright red lingerie
I paused in amazement at how gorgeous she was
I was already in love
She had a landing strip above her Yoni
I thought it was the cutest thing I'd ever seen in my life
I loved it
We made love until we couldn't anymore
It was the first day that I found
Home

## Dear Immanuel 14SEP19

Last night I dropped you back off to your mother
I cried tries of sorrow
It hurt knowing that tomorrow I would wake up and you
wouldn't be next to me
Today I posted pictures of you to Instagram
Before people would always ask me why I didn't or if I was
ashamed or not proud of you
But the truth is I was having my own internal conflict
As if I wasn't your father
As if I didn't deserve to be your father
As if my own transgressions have stripped me of the ability to
say that I love you too
So today I posted you
And it felt right

## To tell the truth

I just want to hold you again

## Ignorance

I have been condemned for crimes that I never committed
People have written me off without hearing my side of the story
I sit in silence
Pretend like the harsh reality of the pain doesn't ache my spine
Makes it hard for me to stand up straight
I mask it in my stride
Because a man is supposed to be a man always
Even when he is being mistreated by the people he loves
Even when his friends reveal their companionship only out of convenience
Even when his son doesn't even know that he is his son
Even when the pressure of taking care of three households and two other grown men takes a toll on him
Even when he gains 60 pounds from depression
Even when he sucks up his pride and sees a therapist in private for a year
Even when he has been crying out for help in packed rooms, but nobody seems to hear him scream
Even when one women doesn't want him because he's too "perfect" for her
And the next because he isn't good enough
Even when he's alone
All of the time. No friends. No family. No lover.
Just the four walls of his studio apartment
Everyday
Even when silence is too loud
He is supposed to be a man
Suck that shit up and do not fold
Stay ten toes down behind your existence
Be still with your choices
Ignore your pain
Be a real man

## Dear Immanuel, 13JAN19

Today I tried to kill my self
Selfish of me I know
But honestly, I didn't see the purpose of me being around
You were in a better situation without me
Your mother smiled in ways she never did with me
You both looked complete
And I was banned from your life
No matter how hard I would try
It was never good enough
Thankfully the universe didn't agree with my depression
By some miracle
I survived
It had to have been for **you.**